MESHUGGENAH

A UNIQUE COLLECTION OF POEMS

AL HOLTZMAN MAGRATH

MESHUGGENAH

Paperback First Edition 2020

Published by AL Holtzman Magrath, St. Louis MO

Email: alexm0400@gmail.com

Credits:
Graphic Design by Elaine A. Young, hopdezin@swbell.net
www.hopscotchcommunications.com

About the Author

I've been writing for 15 years. Writing more seriously for the last ten years. I started writing poetry more consistently over the last year, and have written about 145 poems in that time. I'm a musician as well and have been for 15 years. I play the guitar, sing, and rap. I've played shows around the St. Louis area for the last 15 years. I started writing more seriously during my senior year of high school. I attended a national competition for slam poetry in San Francisco when I was eighteen. Our team from University City High School placed 5th out of forty teams in that competition. Since I've posted my poems online over the last year, I have gotten about 20,000 views on my poetry. I am a senior political science major at Webster University in St. Louis, MO.

Acknowledgments

I would like to thank my mother and father, Linda Holtzman and Mike Magrath for being constant supportive forces of love in my life. I'd like to thank Dominic Geinosky Pioter for opening the door to poetry in my life as a great teacher during my senior year of high school in 2005 at University City High School. I'd like to thank David Clewell for being a constant poetic inspiration in my life over the years since I took a poetry class from him at Webster University in 2005. I'd like to thank Tabitha Humphrey for being an inspiration and force of creative good in my life since 2004, particularly opening the door for me to the vast world of poetry. I'd like to thank my sister, Dora Holtzman Magrath, for forever being in my heart and with me in spirit. I'd like to thank my sisters Sheila Miranda and Bernadette Magrath Brown for being loving and supportive over the years through thick and thin. And finally, I'd like to thank Rabbi James Stone Goodman for his consistent support and inspiration over the last 15 years of my life. I owe my life to the rabbi in many ways, and he as inspired me as a fellow poet.

The Matrix and Mental Health

The matrix is an
Interesting concept.
We might live in one.
A lot of people think
They're Neo.
Most of these people
Are mentally ill.
I used to think I
Was the messiah.
Mental illness is
No joke.
I've been through a lot.
Medicine helps.
I'm relieved to not
Be a savior.
I'm just a regular guy.
I only say that because
I don't believe there is
Such a thing as a
Regular guy.
It is possible to appear
As a regular kind of guy
And be an eccentric
At the same time.
There is a spectrum of
Weirdness just like in

Any other category.
Being a savior would
Be too much work.
The amount of stress
I felt when I believed this
Delusion was immense.
It is part of what landed
Me in a psych ward
Many times.
Many many times.
I just like being a crazy
poet/musician/writer.
I like being a human
Being with strengths
And weaknesses.
Vulnerability is viewed
As weakness but it is
Really a strength.
Empowering.
Truth is often vulnerable.
I'm just – AJ Holtzman Magrath
and
That is enough.

SHADES OF BLUE

I'm sitting in a
Living room looking at
Different shades
Of blue.
Some red.
Some purple.
I have nothing
Wise to say.
My surroundings are
Meditative.
There is always
Potential for peace
But I don't feel
Peaceful.
I've got a lot of
Homework.
School is kicking my ass.
I'm sick of talking
About school.
I'm sick of being
IN school.
Yet I push forward.
It's the only way that
Is acceptable to me.
And the different

Shades of blue
Calm me.
Some purple.
Some red.
They are calming.
There are loads of stress
On my back but I find
Solace in persisting.
Persistence is key.
And hard work.
And more rest.
The sky is overcast
But I am still here.
I feel internal brightness
Amidst the darkness,
The depression.
I will succeed.
I am a writer.
Hopefully I have said
Something here that
Will help somebody.
Be present amidst the
Colors surrounding you.
That is always a blessing.

6

The Sun is My Hope

The sun is my hope.
My hope is the sun.
I'm afraid of failure
But more afraid of success.
Success is sometimes
Nothing more than
Keeping it together for
A bunch of days.
Doing your best.
Sometimes more than that.
Sometimes less.
Sometimes right on the money.
I needed a break today
So I took it.
No homework.
Falling behind.
One step back,

Two steps forward.
I'm writing and getting rest.
The sun is my hope but
Emptiness is king.
Who would've thought
That life would be this
Paradoxical and complex.
Keep it simple stupid.
I'm so smart that I'm dumb
And vice versa.
Or maybe I'm just a regular guy.
The sun is my hope.
My hope is the sun.
It's time to succeed.
Taking care of oneself
Is the most important thing.

Hopeful Mans Van Gogh

Writing feels like
Skipping across a
Pond into the distance.
I love water.
Lily pads and impressionist
Paintings.
Monet and Van Gogh.
Vincent wasn't appreciated
In his life time.
What does that say about
The worlds ability to
Judge what is sacred and beautiful?
My fate is within reach as I
Skip across the pond.
This life is like a Van Gogh painting.
Beautiful and tragic.
Holy.

Money isn't everything
But I could use a little
Bit of recognition.
I'd prefer perfection of my
Craft over anything else.
I would sacrifice
Everything for that.
I think I already have.
Could I be the Van Gogh of
My generation?
Hopefully just a little less
Tragic.
I could be the hopeful mans
Van Gogh.
But for now I'll just rest
On my lily pad
For the evening
And enjoy the view.

Just An Alcoholic

I'm a lone shark.

I'm a lone saint.

I'm just an alcoholic.

I'm climbing mountains

Every time I study.

If they're just small hills

Then why do they seem so high?

Maybe I'm dramatic.

Maybe I'm unfulfilled.

When I'm climbing

In the act of study

The distance seems moot.

I build the distance up

In my head.

It would be helpful to

Be less dramatic.

Its not that important.

Or isn't it?

I'm just an alcoholic with

A flair for writing.

Or maybe I've got something

here.

Or maybe both.

A powerful paradox.

What makes me

Original?

The flair, the drama,

Plus whatever talent

I possess is a potion for

Excellence.

Theres something to be

Hopeful for, for sure.

I need the world to applaud

My poetry because

Its never enough

And I'm just an

Alcoholic.

An alcoholic with

Seven months sober.

Among the Living

I am almost caught up
In my classes.
What a lovely day.
Except for getting a citation
On the metrolink for not
Having a card for my
Reduced fair pass.
And missing a meeting
With my friend who is also
The chair of the political science/
International relations/history
Department at Webster University
In St. Louis, Mo. where I attend classes.
But I made it on time to both of my classes,
American Politics and French and took a quiz
For each of the classes.
I did better on American Politics than French.
But I get to retake the French quiz on Friday

So we're all good.

I went to my home group and dinner with

My sponsor and other friends of Bill's

Tonight.

That was really nice.

Good food and company at Michaels.

I hate that my sponsor has to pay for me.

But he doesn't mind.

I mind, but it's ok for now.

I'm making major moves.

Being sober is a blessing.

I've come back from the dead.

Rejoined the living.

Become a part of the human

Race again.

Even the citations are beautiful

In a pain in the ass way.

Overall, it was a good day.

More Than a Dream

I'm hopeful and depressed.
Mainly hopeful.
The sky asks me questions.
I have no answer except
To get closer.
Touching the sky is more
Than a dream.
If only I could feel
The air the way
That I feel the oceans blue.
It's touch is unattainable.
That is part of its appeal.
I can feel the air but
I want to feel the sky.
One can still hope.
Hope is like the sky.

Touching the sky is
More than a dream.
I'm getting closer every day.
My persistence is a
Shade of blue.
I'm getting closer.
The more I persist,
The more I awake.
Persistence is the key
To touching what can only
Be felt in ones
Imagination.
Persistence is the sky.
I can touch it.
It's more than a dream.

A Drop in the Ocean and Yellow Labs

A drop in the ocean
Is the color blue.
My salvation comes
One drop at a time.
Thank God for that
Paradox.
My dog is my cross.
Thank God for dogs
And vice versa.
Yellow labs make the
World taste good.
Life is but a stream of knowledge…
And infinite everything else.
My yellow lab is named Juno.
Some think she's named after
The capitol of Alaska,
Some say the movie,
Some say the Greek goddess.
Truth is she's named after the
Movie.

But she breathes force
Into my life more strongly
Than all of the Greek
Gods combined.
She loves water.
She loves to swim.
My dog.
The ocean.
The color blue.
Three life long loves.
She's 12.
I'll be devastated when
She goes.
To many more years.
To many more swims.
To many more drops
In the ocean.
Long live Juno
And this thing
Called Life.

It Has Begun

School Just Started
This week.
Stressful but not impossible
By any means.
It's going to take a lot of
Inner and outer work
Simultaneously.
French language, American Politics,
And Senior Overview.
My soul is not completely
Interested in the subject
Material.
It's only a means to an end.
I'm somewhat interested
But it feels forced.
The degree will lead me
toward clinical psychology
In graduate school.
What a beautiful and tough
Conundrum.
But I know I'm lucky to be able
To take these classes,
And for free at that.
These are high quality classes
At Webster University.
Classes are stressful but I'm
Blessed, thankful, and
Ready to work hard.

A Beautiful Day

The love of a lifetime
Sanctified all of the
Struggle.
It was overcast today
But extremely sunny
In spirit.
A lovely day.
Hung out with my
Wonderful father.
We went to a St. Louis
University women's
Basketball game and
They lost.
But the pep band was great
And it feels like we won.
School starts tomorrow
And I'm a little nervous
But not too bad.
My dogs poop was normal
Today.

I got my medicine that
I needed and my
Lovely dad offered to pay
My overdue rent so I don't
Have to sell my last guitar.
He paid for my medicine too.
The sky is overcast but
I haven't seen a cloud in the sky
All day.
Like Ice Cube said, "Today was a
good day."
I feel the light giving heat of the
sun
Though I didn't see the yellow
ball
All day.
Everything looks a lot better.
Thank God for my father.

6 Months Sober

I had 6 months sober 2 days ago.
It feels good.
I was at a pretty weird meeting today.
People were acting strange.
Cross talking and speaking somewhat
Inappropriately.
It got more inappropriate as the
Meeting dragged along.
Someone was there who was sold
Fentanol from someone at the
Lindell Club where the meeting was.
This was rather scary.
Life can be scary sometimes.
Someone had almost died from an
Overdose as a result.
He wasn't breathing for 5 minutes.
Scary stuff.
It reminded me of what my life was like
Before I got sober.
I overdosed on pills a couple of times
And didn't think I was going to survive.
And now I'm thriving.
6 months sober and
I'm grateful for where I'm at.
Extremely grateful.
Things are very different than
They were 6 months ago.
Blessings rain down.

100 Stressful Days

Turquoise is a beautiful
Color.
I wish my life was that
Shade of blue.
I'm trying to make it
That way.
I'm trying to bend my life
Towards my own justice.
But I'm very nervous about
Shool starting Monday.
I have a spotty past with
School.
I'm going to try to do
Better this time.
The sky is overcast today.
So is my soul.
Anxiety reigns supreme.

I feel like I'm losing my
Creative, poetic energy.
I feel like I'm writing the
Same shit over and over again.
Exhausted by the bliss of
100 stressful days.
Maybe 1,000.
Maybe 10,000.
My life has been a lovely
Picture of anxiety.
Maybe not so lovely.
Maybe not so blissful.
But I'm still here.
It hasn't always been this
Stressful.
It's all going to be okay.

Depression Did Not Break Me

Depression is a rock.
It's there for you when
No one else is.
But I'm tired of that friend.
Yet my dark friend has come
To talk with me again.
I'm tired of school.
A monolith of regret.
An unstoppable force of
Nervousness.
My solidity in frame
Is diminishing.
But my soul is
Unconquerable.
Thank the Spirit for that.
I've been through many
Worse periods of time.

Times that almost broke me.
But I did not break.
If I can get through those times,
I can get through these.
Spirit of the Universe,
Give me the strength to
Achieve my dreams.
I'm prepared to do
Whatever is necessary
to successfully complete
This semester.
Give me strength
And grant me serenity.
Spirit of the Universe,
You are my true rock.
Not my depression.

The Pain is Fierce

The pain I'm in is fierce.
I have to sell my guitar to pay
For my rent.
My last guitar that I have.
Times are tough.
Writing is my only solace.
I'm nervous.
I start school on Monday.
Getting back on the hamster
Wheel.
I hope this isn't the beginning
Of another fuck up.
I know I can do it.
But the pain I'm in is fierce.
I hope I will succeed.
Its been an up and down journey.
A long and winding road.
My determination is as fierce
As my doubts.
I have always been persistent.
Even amidst my setbacks.
I never give up.
I won't ever give up.
I refuse.
My soul is undefeated.
Thank God for hope.
A gorgeous melody.
I will always listen,
Even when the demons
Raise hell.
The pain I'm in is fierce.
But You are more fierce,
And so am I.

Its Raining Buckets

Its raining buckets in
Midtown St. Louis.
I feel like I have
Nothing to say.
My old friend came to
My moms place tonight.
The three of us had
A great talk.
But in the end I was
Embarrassed about the
Way my life turned out.
In a way, rain is fitting
For the night.
I walked home in it
With a measly umbrella
And my dog had a bad case
Of diarrhea.
I'm hurt inside.
These poems are becoming
Prose.

I guess that's fitting since
Much of my prose sounds
Like poetry.
I'm hurt inside.
I don't like the way my life
Turned out.
There is more to come.
Thats part of what I'm afraid of.
Changing my life around feels
Like a lot of pressure.
But it can be done.
And I've already changed much
Of it around already.
Silver lining.
It's raining buckets outside.
The weather goes well
With my mood.

A WINTERS EMBRACE

A winters embrace.
The cold is beautiful.
I'm glad I'm not homeless.
These people seem
Miserable
Out in the cold.
I would be too.
Newport tobacco in my lungs.
Nicotine too.
And whatever else.
Cancer not yet formed.
I hope to quit soon.
I kind of care.
Kind of don't care.
My candles are
Shining light
As I write.
I've been up since 4:30 am.
Oh beautiful life,
Why are you so cruel
And ample with blessings?
Existential pain abounds.
Existential hope reigns as
Victor.
I have a Dr. Viktor Frankl
Kind of hope.
These are dark times but
I'm finding meaning in them.

Seriously Comical

Seriously comical

It was good to go

To a meeting tonight.

There is strength

In persistence.

A beautiful love/hate story.

That's why we go

Sometimes-

To get inspiration from others.

Experience can get you a long way,

Especially when you learn it

From others.

Others who have more time and...

Experience.

Faith can be found as

Easily as it is

Lost.

Love is just hate turned

Inside out.

It is made of the same

Stuff.

It is as complex as its

Differences.

Love is a serious game.

Seriously Comical
It was good to go
To a meeting tonight.
There is strength
In persistence.
A beautiful love/hate story.
That's why we go
Sometimes-
To get inspiration from others.
Experience can get you a long way,
Especially when you learn it
From others.

Others who have more time and...
Experience.
Faith can be found as
Easily as it is
Lost.
Love is just hate turned
Inside out.
It is made of the same
Stuff.
It is as complex as its
Differences.
Love is a serious game.

Good Luck Demons

A lovely day.
A chill in the air.
My ghost is gone
But my spirit isn't.
My soul flies out
Of my body for visits
To the 7th dimension,
Then returns to my
Body faithfully.
My energy is not done
Yet on this Earth.
I'm full of fight.
I'm not going down easily.
No one is trying to take
Me down that I'm aware of,
Except for my own internal
Demons.
These are the hardest foe
To defeat.
I'm my own worst enemy
And my own best friend.
This is a dialectic that I
Cannot escape,
Nor would I want to.
I like the battle. I like the fight.
I like the war.
Paradoxically, the challenge
Brings me peace.
My soul is unconquerable.
Good luck demons.

LIKE A VESSEL

My love is like a vessel
Out to sea.
The storm is intense.
I see no other boat on the horizon.
But I can feel its pull.
I hope my life mate
Will come running,
Or sailing, more accurately.
My love is like a vessel out to sea.
Its lonely but the storm
Is what has made me who I am.
Perhaps the bad weather will end
And I will find my most important
Lover who also survived the winds.
How lovely are life's challenges.
Silently cursing them
But they made me.
Long live the storm.
And John Lennon.

WRITERS BLOCK

I have a severe case of
Writers block.
I'm having trouble with what to write.
I still love writing but
I don't know what to say.
A poem about not knowing
What to write.
How original.
My love is like a bird
Without wings to fly.
The art of writing helps
Me to rebuild
My wings to take flight again.
My essence is like an
Empty vessel,
Still afloat.
My writing is similar.
Poetry is my long lost love.
My love is like a caged bird
That cannot fly.
Creativity is my wings.
Now I need a key to get
Out of the cage.
Now I know, as Ms. Angelou
Said, why the caged bird sings.
It's because I am that bird.
I'm grateful for my voice
I feel free when I sing.
When I sing, I get lost in each
Moment of time
With freedom.
So why am I shy?
Beautiful bliss.
How lovely life is, even with
A jam in the pipe of
Creativity.

An Old Friend

I got together with an old friend tonight.
It was really good to see him.
He said, "Its funny the way things
Turn out, isn't it?"
I agreed.
Although it hasn't been as
Comedic for me.
I love my friend and know he
Didn't mean any harm.
But still, funny isn't exactly the
Way I would put it.
It was just this summer
That I was delusional,
Overdosed on pills,
And was overall fighting for my life.
But things are a lot better now.
And he didn't know what I'd been through.
In some ways, it is funny how things turned out.
But it will be a lot more comedic
Once I start making money
From my poetry book and my memoir.
I felt the love though for my old friend.
Its actually my young friend
as he would have me put it.
It was lovely to see him.
A good friend forever and always,
Even if we don't talk for stretches of time.
A great guy.
We all deserve a little humor
In our lives.

Fly as High as You Fall

What to write about?
The green eye of jealousy?
The golden eye of a king?
Much anticipated freedom
For you and me?
I want freedom so badly
I can taste it in its texture.
Writing past dark but
It's only 7:10 pm.
Freedom tastes like the
Paper that I'm writing on.
My freedom is made of ink and
trees.
I'm pouring out my heart into
The page like an unhinged
Philosophy.
A maniacal healer,
Hoping for healing
With every word, every line.
May we all find some sanity.
It is my hope that my poetry might
Move you like a drop of rain
falling
Off of a leaf, naturally.
Surviving the mean streets
Of St. Louis City.
Experiencing misery in Missouri.
May your tears flow naturally.
Or your smiling laughter.
Or both.

Whatever is real for you.
My stomach knots in pain.
I'm not sick.
Just emotional.
And a little sick mentally.
But I like it that way.
There's a thin line between
Insanity and controversial genius.
I'm not saying I'm a genius.
Just suggesting it.
I can only fly as high in happiness
as
I can fall in depression.
Oh how I love Carl Jung.
We're at war with Iran.
That's all I'm going to say
About that.
The world is allowing us many
New present moments.
It would be good if we could
Stop fucking it up so much.
I'm just going to keep trying
To do better.
If you're depressed, just
remember
That you can fly as high
As you fall.
Love, AJ

BACK HOME

I'm back home at Icon.
The first time in a long time that
I've written at my own desk.
It feels lovely.
My room is a mess.
I'll get it organized in time.
This is certainly the life of
A starving artist/writer.
I hope it will all be worth
It in the end.
Doing what you love is
Always worth it,
No matter the outcome.
I still haven't found the
Bonnie to my Clyde.
I'm surrounded by books.
Hundreds of them.
I love that.
It's taken a long time of persistent
Book collecting to reach
This many books in
My possession.
I found a book called
Writing past dark

That I've been looking for
awhile.
I'm excited to read it.
I just finished a book called
The Right to Write.
I love reading books on writing-
I'll take creative inspiration
And knowledge on writing
Wherever I can get it.
I love writing like I hope
God loves me.
I'm listening to classical music
By Chopin as I write.
How lovely.
I feel very hopeful.
I also feel sad.
But more hopeful than sad.
Thank The Spirit for writing.
For better or worse,
I'm at my own desk.
It feels pretty good.
For better or worse,
I'm back home.

MONEY IS A KILLER

Money is a killer.
At least for me.
I don't have enough of it.
Or maybe I can't live
Within my means.
It's hard to live within
Your means when the means
Is only 1, 000 dollars a month.
I know many people have
Less than that.
I should be grateful.
Is it possible to be grateful
And also hope for more?
And also acknowledge that
I have a problem with
Frivolous spending?
I'm tired of fucking up.
I'm tired of being broke.
Responsible money management
Eludes me.
I don't know what to do.
Money is a killer.
Or maybe the killer is not having
Enough of it.
I'm tired of being broke.
Fiscal impulsivity is a problem.
I hope I can overcome this.
I won't give up.
Cheers to the hope of
Better tomorrows.

A Lovely Day

It's been a lovely day.
A chill in the air.
Very few clouds in the sky.
The sky is speaking volumes.
Sky blue sky.
The color meets with the
Chill like long lost brothers.
I was waiting on the bus.
Saw my friend Lester.
Had a good talk.
Happy to wait in the
relationship
Between temperature and
color.
The atmosphere is kind.
Looks like the world
Will survive another 24 hours.
It's been a lovely day.

ST. LOUIS BLUES

Here come the St. Louis
Blues again.
Not the hockey team.
Although they're doing well.
Nothing feels funny.
I guess that's why all I want
To do is laugh.
What I would trade
For a good belly laugh.
Or maybe a good belly cry.
Or both.
Maybe Kevin Hart, Dave Chappelle,
Or Louis CK will do the trick.
Grand Blvd is a ghost town in an empty
Small city on a forgotten Friday.
Everyone is recuperating
From Christmas.
I do live in the Bible Belt.
And in a drinking town.
Sadness is like a lasso grabbing
My life force by the hand of an
Old, formidable foe.
I get comfort from Aaron Trotter
When he raps, "My brain pours water
Out my tear ducts to heal me."
When I can't let myself heal in this way
I get comfort from Shawn Carter when he raps,
"I can't see em coming down my eyes,
So I gotta make the song cry."
So I'll make the poem cry.
It's an emotional purgatory when the tears
Won't flow.
So until then, I'm stuck with the St. Louis
Blues again.

DARKNESS SETS IN

Darkness sets in.
An old friend.
A spiritual lullaby.
A forgotten rehearsal for
Nothing.
Depth personified.
I won't ever stop trying
Until the day I die.
Lovely poems stretched
From a dense, microscopic
Depression.
Bang! Goes the infinite
Emotional abyss.
I will always be devoted.
Where is my savior?
At the end of the day
I guess that is my job.
Jesus didn't die for me.
But I think John Lennon did.
Black clouds cry watery tears.
Downpours of hope amidst
Undeniable atmospheric pressure.
Darkness sets in.

"_____"
Love is an empty concept.
How much greater could
It be if the sentiment was not
Tyrannically ruled by the word
Itself.
What is love without the word?
Could it be called something
else?
What is the meaning of the word
Without all of the hopeful
And heartbreaking stories
associated
With it?
What is "love?"
I ask earnestly.
Perhaps I could tolerate it
More without the sickening
Recollections of all of the
Beautiful and dreadful
History or the sound associated
With its name.
Perhaps I could tolerate it more
If my parents hadn't gotten
A divorce.
Or if my first girlfriend
Hadn't broken up with me

On Valentine's Day and broken
my finger
In a fight we had.
Or if my sister hadn't expressed
Her affection for me
Then hooked up with my friend
And then shot herself,
Leaving a great wake of
emotional scars.
Or if "it" didn't seem fake.
Or if I wasn't disgusted
At the superficial nature of so
many
Relationships between people
Claim to be in "_____."
Or if my ex hadn't left me
High and dry after my sister died.
Or if my most recent ex hadn't
expressed
Hers for me
And then emotionally abuse me
After I began to leave her.
Or if I wasn't alone.
Or if...maybe if I were in "_____,"
Then it would all make sense.
Long live "_____," whatever
That...is.

What Dora Did

My sister died in 2008.
She killed herself.
Shot to the head.
For years I
Did not want to live.
And simultaneously did not
Want to do to my family
What she did.
She destroyed us when
She destroyed herself.
Not wanting to live,
Not wanting to die.
This is a special kind of hell.
Perhaps purgatory.
When she took her life,
She saved mine.
She showed me what suicide
Does to the people
Left behind.

This carried me through much
Darkness of life and mind.
I saw the act she took
In my dreams.
Her funeral was the day before
My 21st birthday.
Every year I struggle with
The catch 22 of her death
juxtaposed
With the celebration of my birth.
But I'm done with the darkness.
I'll always love and miss my
sister,
But I've been through enough.
I haven't gotten over her death.
But I've learned how to live
without her.
And this year I choose to
celebrate.

I Too Know The Darkness

I too know the darkness.
The darkness that shines
The only light.
I spent years in that
Solitary hole.
Depression is a great teacher.
I needed to understand the
Darkness before I could
Truly see the sky, blue with hope.
I came out of the solitary hole
Not unscathed.
I will always know the darkness.
A true friend.
And as a result,
I now know the light.

SACRED SYMBOLS

I can feel the energy
Of my jewelry.
Just like my poetry.
Amythest, Onyx, Citrine,
and Turquoise.
They're calling my future
To meet with the
Present moment.
Destiny- come forth and
Show yourself.
I'm ready.
Stones of my sacred
Hope.
Symbols bearing witness
To the arc of my dreams.
Never forget them.
Dr. King said, "The arc of
History bends toward
Justice."
I will make my own
Justice.
I will make history
Every day.
The stones speak a truth
Unfathomable to translate.
Come on arc.
Bring it home.
Sacred Symbols.
Sacred journey.
Sacred life.
Arc of justice.
Dreams.
Never forget.
Never give in.
Never give up.

Never Been Peter Pan

I'm undone.
I've grown up.
Sometimes I grow wings
When I write.
Incomplete.
A starving artist.
An orphan of thought.
Where is my tinker bell?
Though I love life,
I've never been Peter Pan.
Sometimes my life don't love me.
I wish I could fly.
Sometimes I grow wings
When I write.
Long live writing.
Long live the orphan who
Never became Peter Pan.

DIALECTICAL DREAM

Darkness sets in.
The light of classical music
Pierces the black as the
Brightness of the written word
Penetrates the page.
A gorgeous dichotomy.
A dialectical dream.
2020 comes crashing in
Peacefully like a perfect catch-22.
I will make this year
Great if it kills me.
No resolution except to keep
Doing what I'm doing
Only better.
This night is lonely
Only because I want it to be.
I'm satisfied.
Despite the aching pain of
Emptiness.
I feel whole.
Just me and my writing,
The way it should be.

BLUE SKY BLUE

I love the color blue.
The tranquil sound of
The ocean with its waves.
The silent epoch of the sky.
Its immensity surrounds us
Thinning into nowhere.
A beautiful royal blue sports car.
The paint shining back at the sun.
Surrounding the sky blue
clouds from the ground.
Atmospheric illusivity.
Sea blue with the dolphins.
A color that sounds as good
As it looks.
The ice cold touch of water and
Wind flowing through your fingertips
as
Your hand folds.
The undeniable color of anyone
that sees relatively speaking.
A color that can be seen and unseen.
It can be felt and dreamed.
I do love the color blue.

LISTEN TO THE AMETHYST ROCK

What inspires when
Creatively one hears nothing?
This is the time to listen.
Listen to the colors.
Listen to the sounds.
Feel the Amethyst Rock
Resting on your heart,
Crying toward a deep laughter.
Laughing through empty tears.
Experience all of the senses,
Not in any particular order.
No matter what,
Continue to listen,
Even if it means touching
Or seeing the sound.
I like to listen to the Amethyst Rock.

Free the Mentally ILL

I'm not my mental illness.
How do I accept my mental
illness
Without being a victim?
You tell me I'm responsible for
My behavior but I know that's
incomplete.
I take medicine to help my
Behavior, to help my thinking,
And to help me make better
Choices as a result.
I'm doing better
But when I slip up,
I am still blamed.
You blame me,
But you don't blame a cancer
patient
When their cancer comes out of
remission.
How will we overcome this
victim-blaming?
We can start by knowing that
there's a thin line between
insanity and controversial genius.

The good is connected to the
bad.
If you can realize that
My genius, the things you praise
me for,
Are connected to the things you
blame me for,
My illness, then you can learn to
To give me more of a break
When you're own impulse is to
judge my faults
But praise my gifts,
When it is all connected.
Free the mentally ill.
We suffer enough without
your additional blame and guilt.
Free the Mentally ill.
I'm more than my illness.
Free the Mentally ill.
If not now then when?
Free the Mentally ill.
If not me then who?
We will overcome.

The Muddy Mississippi

I see the arch in the distance.
As I contemplate my future.
I feel the residue of tomorrow
And the freshness of today.
The arch is lit up on the
Muddy Mississippi and
I'm growing.
A poem written daily.
I want inner peace and the
Wisdom to not take
Myself so seriously.
Over and out.

The Right to Write

Ultimately, I write because
I like to write.
I like the act of writing.
I like thinking of the
next line I'm going to write
that will work with the
previous lines and the overall
scope and future lines of the poem.
It doesn't cost anything to write,
for which I'm thankful.
The more I write,
the more likely it will be
published and bought.
So I suppose it's great that
I love the act of writing.
I'm thankful for having
the right to write.
I'm glad that I love writing.
This is my 22nd poem
that I'll upload onto www.allpoetry.com.
I'm getting closer to having enough poems
to make a poetry book.
This may not be the greatest poem
I've ever written,
But I have the right to write,
and no matter the outcome,
I'm glad I took advantage of it.
Everything you write isn't
going to be your best.
But I wrote another poem,
for which I'm grateful.

Bamboo and Jasmine Symphony

I'm sitting in a chair
Next to a Bamboo and Jasmine
Scented candle, thinking
Of my poetic symphony.
Each of these words
Represents a different note.
I don't know what will
Be my masterpiece.
But I feel the diversity of
The notes as they leave my brain
And are printed on the page.
Some symphonies are
Extremely simple- some
Are extremely complex.
Most are probably somewhere
In between.
Perhaps the practice, each
New poem written, each letter
Each note, is a building block to
An eventual symphonic masterpiece.
I like the act of writing. I suppose
That is most important in the present.
As I smell the bamboo and Jasmine,
The scent burning into the air,
I contemplate my poetic symphony.
My eventual masterpiece,
But am satisfied with the diverse notes
That make up every poem like the poets
of past, present, and future.
I am overwhelmed with the sense of being
Exactly where I need to be.

45

THE MAN FROM NOWHERE

I spoke to the man
from nowhere.
there was no successful
translation.
maybe this is like the
distance between Faith
and Heaven.
what if all of our efforts
to understanding the Spirit World
were lost in translation?
this non-discovery of a
discovery could be the best
thing that ever happened
to humankind.
never overlook the ones
from nowhere.

The Snow

The snow was beautiful.
It is no longer fresh.
Why do things become spoiled
And appeal less to us?
Why don't I like dirty snow?
I don't understand the nature
Of ugliness and beauty.
I broke up with a girl because
I wasn't attracted to her.
Such a impactful response born from
A superficial drive that I don't believe in.
Yet we like what we like.
The snow was beautiful.
But what is the beauty beyond
The tainted nature of time?
I want to love the dirt in the snow.
Are we not all snowdrifts
aging like fine wines trying to
Purify our dirt as we fade away?
I want a love like that
And a woman who's easy on the eyes.

If Only A Channel

Insert something deep here.
What wants to be written
Through me?
Is that how it works?
How do I find my ideal
Of writing that is best-suited
For me?
Maybe it's trial and error.
I'm sure that's part of it.
If I'm only a channel for Higher Thought,
Then what am I?
Originality is very rare.
Most breakthroughs are
Simply old ideas reorganized in New ways.
I'm on the cusp of something
Relatively new perhaps.
I question deeply in my mine of thought.
If only a channel, what am I?
A purposeless drone?
A misunderstood genius?
A regular person?
All of the above?
I don't have any concrete answers.
Perhaps my poems are puzzle pieces
That only make sense within
The context of my larger body of work.
At the end of the day,
I hope I have said something that helps.

An Oddball Kind of Love

Love is a losing game.
That has been true for me.
Hopefully not for the rest of my life.
As long as I still believe in love.
Sometimes it feels like love
Involves being cliche.
As much as I hate that,
I still love love enough to
weather that storm.
Or maybe I don't know
What love is..
Love love love.
Blah blah blah.
A general self hate encompasses
My "self" as I write the word love
And talk about it repetitively.
I hate being cliche.
Maybe love isn't cliche.
I want a non-cliche
Kind of love.
But I'll take it in whatever
Form it gives itself.
I want a winning,
Odd ball kind of love.
But until I find it,
Love is still a losing game.

Substance Qualified

I'm lost and found
Multiple times each day.
My hurt is profound
And substanceless.
What is substance?
We think we know
But do we?
Just because you go through
A lot doesn't mean you are filled with substance.
Just because your life has
Been easy doesn't mean you're
Automatically simple or shallow.
There's a lot of suffering amidst
The winds of life's pages as they turn
No matter what you're reading.
Either way,
My soul is full
Of shit
But also
Good Stuff.
I think I could qualify for having
Substance.
I'm a little bit attached to
My suffering,
The ills that have plagued me.
The heaviest load of substance
Can be held without any
Answers.
I don't have the answers
but I do know some things.

Life and War

I love life.
Sometimes I think my life
Don't love me.
I know that is a bunch
Of bullshit.
Life is beyond love.
It is also beneath love,
And right beside it.
I'm looking at a
Picture of my grandpa in
His WW2 soldiers uniform
And think about all of the times
He could've died in the war
But didn't.
I wouldn't be here if he died.
Obviously.
But sometimes it's good to
Realize the heaviness
Of that fact,
The gratitude for life
That it brings.
The things my grandpa
Had to go through and survive
In order that I be blessed with this life.
He sacrificed a lot in order that I live.
I'm grateful.

Anything But Me

I'm tired.
I'm sad.
I'm frustrated.
I feel emotionally
Constipated.
I'm not where I want to be,
The present moment and
It's circumstances.
I'm sick of complaining.
I'm sick and tired of being
Sick and tired.
Cliche I know.
I'm sick of people claiming
They have the answers.
I'm tired of reading all of these great
Books and still feeling like the same
Broken person.
I'm sick of my family being sick of me.
I'm sick of feeling like I have to
Defend my worth.
I'm sick of wondering if I have worth.
I'm sick of burdens.
I'm sick of myself, whoever
That is.
I'm sick of people judging me.
I'm sick of pretending like I don't care.
I'm sick of the haves and the have-nots.
I'm sick of the have-nots having not.
I'm sick of the privileged people who are
Considered successful for all of the
Wrong reasons.
I'm sick of the term successful.
I'm sick of the generic, generalized, capitalistic,
One-sided nature of that

Words definition.
I'm sick of taking life seriously.
I'm sick of other people taking it so lightly.
I'm sick of my imperfections and
Character defects.
I'm sick of pretending like any asshole
Perception of me is the real me.
I'm sick of being told to be positive.
I'm sick of not being positive.
Sometimes I get sick of being positive too.
I'm sick of being negative too.
Sometimes I'm attached to my suffering.
I'm tired of the grey area.
I'm tired of trying to be balanced.
I'm tired of being an undergraduate student
At 32 years old.
I'm tired of trying to be what anyone else
Wants me to be.
I'm tired of feeling I'm not enough
When I am.
Enough for who?
I'm tired of the mainstream
Status quo.
I'm tired of not fitting in.
I'm tired of the title of my upcoming book.
I'm sick of having to be painfully aware
Of everything.
I'm tired of being a
Starving artist and writer.
I'm tired of not loving myself.
I'm tired of caring what you think.
I'm tired of wishing I could be a
Version of me that you would love.
I'm tired of wishing you were a different
Version of you that would love me.

Bitter Release

Callin my name,
Hearing me speak.
The voice I hear,
When I go to sleep.
Thoughts of life,
Running far and meek.
Here's the song,
Bitter Release.
Testing me,
Pain is real.
Thoughts of sin,
Make it hard to feel.
Fading voice,
Screaming out loud.
Bleeding heart,
Still so proud.
Hear the voice,
Calling my name.
My thunder rolls around,
Nobodies to blame.
All these people,
Try to get the best of me.
In so much sin,
All I want and need is purity.

Release me,
From this bullshit.
Fuck you all I'll say it a
Million times and still
Feel raw.
Help me feel,
For another day.
Singin ain't cuttin it,
I'm sick of all this bs today.
So help me to feel,
What's real.
Help me to feel,
What's real in this bitter release,
Oh my bitter, my bitter release.
My bitter, my bitter release.
Fuck all the malpractice doctors.
Fuck Trump and Pence for all
The High Crimes.
Fuck all the people that wanna
hold me down.
Now it's time for me to hold it
down
In a song right now.
It's the song called
"Bitter Release."

Song performed live at:
www.youtube.com/watch?v=pOa2t44a9RQ

54

Black Hole Salvation

The darkness
Wraps itself around me
Like a glove.
A tight essential embrace
Of all that is black,
All that is holy.
Dialectical salvation.
Infinite perspectives.
Hopelessness of a bright future.
Heavy redemption.
Beautiful black
Reaches toward
An abyss of love.
A fateful embrace of the present.
A runaway truck is carrying an
Unstoppable truth.
The paradox of darkness and light.
Will always be.
They are mutually exclusive.
Love is empty.
Emptiness is love.
It wasn't until all was lost that
I found my salvation.

As Bad as it Was

I'm not where I want to be,
But it's not as bad as it was.
I don't really quite feel free,
But it's not as bad as it was.
My soul is still amidst it's imprisoning,
But it's not as bad as it was.
My life is not quite redeemed,
But it's not as bad as it was.
I don't totally believe,
But it's not as bad as it was.
My soul is not quite singing,
But it's not as bad as it was.
My freedom bell is not quite ringing,
But it's not
As bad
As it
Was.

Ode to a Poem

This is an ode to a poem.
This type of poem feels good.
It's like an escape from a dream,
The dream of reality.
Reality never killed the dream;
The dream killed reality.
The game is over.
I want to take a vacation via
A poem.
The beauty of making anything I
Dream come to life.
The poem is an escape, a reality check,
Or anything else you want it to be.
It is yours.
This is an ode to a poem.
May your adventures be great
And set you
Free.

Butterfly in the Dark
(Hip-Hop Lyrics)

Writing rhymes, out of my mind.
Mining this creative mine.
Tryna find the gold inside
Before I run out of time.
It's time to shine.
Fall weathers got me feeling fine.
I've weathered so many figurative
Storms that the darkness feels like
Light.
I'm not writing out of spite.
There's a chip on my shoulder but I
Just want to feed the people with it yet
They won't bite.
Despite all the shit I've been through
My future's looking bright. Keepin these
Rhymes tight.
Like a butterfly coming out of the darkness,
I'll get recognition in due time.
Been lighting the dark for so long that
I'm not used to the sun being fuel for my
Fight.
Bright like a star, chaos in my mind.
Tryna create a hit like it depends on my life.
With all of this strife, it's time to strive for
Great heights.
I put down my knife, and I feel twenty pounds
Light-er.
My music glistens;
I've been in the dark for too long. I'm ready for
Ears to listen.

Jaded Musician

I jammed tonight
in a real studio.
It breathed life into my
jaded musician.
Is there still a chance for
better living?
I'm over the music industry.
My spirit is calloused from
all of the disappointment.
Yet
the pain from all of the
let downs is a prerequisite to
mastery.
I have hope.
There is no failure if you refuse to give up.
I yearn for more.
This is my jaded musician.

BARD COLLEGE CAN GO FUCK ITSELF

Bard College Can Go Fuck Itself

I got a full ride scholarship to Bard College

Out of high school. Called the Presidents Scholarship.

I deserved it- busted my ass in high school.

I thought I was the Messiah- but I still got a 3.0 while there.

I saw a counselor there. Told her about being the Messiah.

She said I needed to be on psych meds. I don't remember

Her name, but I told her she can go fuck herself.

I went on a "leave of absence."

I was gonna come back. For sure. It's 14 years later

and I never went back.

They kept saying I wasn't ready. I appealed my leave 5 times.

Bard College can go fuck itself.

Where was your faith in me then, Leon Botstein, the President of

Bard College, whom the scholarship was named after?

David Shein, the Dean of the Lower College, who supposedly was

Fucking

Female Students back to back, who was supposedly trying to help

me, but let me deteriorate slowly into madness without a care.

Both of you can go fuck yourselves. I want to know. How did I go

AL HOLTZMAN MAGRATH

From being the premier student of the incoming freshman class

To a sick dummy that was never ready to come back?

Could it be stigma of mental illness?

Could it be your superficial interest in the outer, not inner,

Success of your students?

When these poems change society, you will never be

A part of my celebration. You will figuratively die in the

Same way I died to you, when I became a liability.

Bard College, go fuck yourself.

I really mean that, sincerely.

You will never be a part of my success,

When you will inevitably try to take it

One day, or get your

share of its worth/credit.

You're already dead to me.

And may your karma fuck you over

As mightily as your decision to blackball me

Fucked me over.

Bard College, you can go fuck yourself.

And go to hell while you're at it.

With Warm Regards,

Al Holtzman Magrath

The Poem that Changes the World

I want to write the poem that changes the world.
It's cold in my apartment; it's cold in the world.
How can we right all of the wrongs?
Redemption needs to be heavy- that's the stuff
that substance and hope are made of.
I want to write the poem that's going to change the world
but the son of a black woman that I know
was just lynched several months ago in
his back yard in the middle of the city of St. Louis.
People are dying needlessly every day from things
that we could prevent. Addiction, patriarchy, and racism
reign. We live in a police state. I want to write the
poem that changes the world but the world is
hard to change. Since there is so much beauty in the world,
that might not be such a bad thing.
I love autumn, fall leaves, Costa Rica, Israel,
raspberries, ice cream, guitars, watches,
snow, hip-hop, jazz, folk, soul, blues, rock,
Martin Guitars, singing, waterfalls, rainbows,
family, friends, oceans, books, love, hope,
determination, rivers, mountains, change, beauty.
I want to write the poem that changes
the world but the world is already changing,
and simultaneously remaining the same.
Focusing on the good might be the very change
agent I'm looking for. Amen.

I Followed The Truth

I followed the
Truth
and it led me here.
Where
Nothing means
Everything
and everything
means nothing.
Maybe I Should Try
Some
MIDDLE GROUND.

THE COLD WIND BLOWS

I feel the cold wind blow in August of summer
Its 5am
My eyes haven't shut
The mind is wide awake
It's 55 degrees

The words-the space-on this page
Are not enough

The cold wind blows

I sense the sun rising
without seeing it
It's 5:05 am
Another chunk
of time
This is what we call it
The present is presenting itself
As emptiness passes
To the next moment
Time
The cold wind blows and

I'm getting older

Their have been many

present moments.

If they were presents

Why do I feel robbed by their sum?

Bipolar, PTSD, Depression

I only just survived the moments
Not unscathed.
It's a beautiful day
It's 5:10 am
But the cold wind blows as
a chill through my bones
like all of the moments
stolen
from all of my days.
I always wish
something could have changed.

But all of those moments are
gone from view,
and regrets are hard to face.

Bloody Relevance

Bloody relevance.
Touchy irreverance.
Impossible music.
Lovely looting.
Corona teaching.
Will we die?
Neo great depression.
Empty love.
Reality check.
Divine lies.
Irresponsible time.
Covid 19 hates us.
Humans will beat it.
A mind void of hope.
A soul full of life.
Heavy redemption
Coming like a runaway
Truck.
Full on devastation.
Desperate wasting.

Immature love wasted.
Wisdom not basic.
Beautiful wishing
Not phased by this.
Tired of lies
Make me cry.
Feels good to be
Alive.
Soul in hyperdrive.
Ready for bigger things.
Moving forward,
To my past
Waving goodbye.
Always gonna try.
Always gonna fight.
Rhyming can be a
Prison.
Fuck.
Shit.
Please help us.
I'm done with this
Stupid fucking poem.
Peace.

From Zero to Nothing Real Fast

What if your high opinion of your knowledge
Meant nothing?

What if your life's work was not your calling?

My friend told me that our conversations didn't
Go anywhere.

I asked her, where are you trying to go?

I thought there was value in deep conversation.

In my mind, I search Heaven, Hell, The Universe, the Earthly plane,

My mind, my soul, reasons for life, philosophy, psychology,

All to find a reason, a motivation, something, anything,

something real.

Healing.

I'm back. I'm 32 years old. Not a college graduate.

I take the bus.

I'm not an established writer or musician.

Sleeping in a messy room. I bought 4 watches. An expensive cologne.
Two pairs of Yeezy's. A pair of Lebron's.

They didn't ease the pain. They didn't fill the void of black.

They didn't make me feel purity or loved.

Maybe she was right.

Maybe I've been wrong all this time.

All of those books. All of that time spent reading,

Writing-thinking-imagining-feeling

Was in vain.

I go to thousands of places in my mind. You say its nowhere.
I Disagree.

If zero is nothing,

Doesn't that make it something?

The Girl With the Standing Vibration

The angels called and sent the healing down.
She stood in the crowd.
She was standing there silently.
Her language was not linguistic.
She did not come to teach.
The president was dirty.
He saw purity, resigned himself to defeat.
He and Congress came to blows.
Blow by blow.
Then people came by the masses.
Blow by blow the violence came to a head.
Then the people left, fed up with the harassment.
The president stood there laughing.
No one could overcome the man who created such madness.
Her eyes met his.
His eyes met hers.
Both held worlds and then a vortex appeared,
Defying reality.
His eyes on the stage,
Hers down in the crowd.
Turns out power is somewhere,
Everywhere, and nowhere.
It's just not where it seems.
Maybe its like Tinker Bell,
To see you first have to believe.
Cuz true power is with the people,

But the people don't feel free.
Could it be in the eyes of her dreams?
Is it where we go when we go to sleep?
Do we really know anything?
Is it even worth questioning?
Then I look at her reveal the skeleton of a man,
Who's power wasn't real,
Without saying a thing.
I still hear the angels message loud and clearly,
And they're vibration is everything- its in my ears.
Cuz I saw a small girl defeat a substanceless fiend.
She was beautiful.
Where does power go?
What is real to you?
You can't choose the truth
If you're truth ain't true.
Picasso said anything you can imagine is proof.
I don't know if his message is 100% true.
But people look up to Picasso, and I do too.
Today I saw a girl topple a dictator;
Who knows where the power will travel to?
But today I saw the standing vibration,
And the people will too.

The End of the World

Who knew that the end of the
world
would be like this?
Nobodies screaming or
jumping out of buildings.
No one is being killed
by police-
at least not in the public eye.
There is no World War III.
There is no murder.
There is no rape.
There is no suicide.
There is just silence.
There is just silence.
There is just silence.
What do you hear?
What do you feel?
What do you see?
I see a ghost town.
I feel extreme anxiety.
But all I hear is silence
and the music on my computer.
My computer cannot drown
out all of the noise.
Silence is deafening.
Who knew that the end of the
world
would be like this?

Going out silently.
We're going to make it through.
But perhaps this is how the
world
will end when it does.
A silent panic.
A soft drowning.
A water filling
up our lungs
in a polluted stupor
of covid virus.
Distance from one another.
Keep 6 feet away.
No hugs.
No handshakes.
No kisses.
No love.
Just distance.
Just distance and
silence.
If I die I will go out with
hope and a cigarette
in my mouth.
We're going to make it.
But who knew that
the worlds end would be
the sound of silence.

NOT GONNA END

The world
Is not
Going
To
End.
Chill
Out.

SEE LIKE STEVIE

love is blind
but Stevie Wonder
can see better
than anyone with
20/20 vision
all I want is freedom
but sometimes i can
barely see
i wish i could see
like Stevie
moral compass
unmatched
when you can love
your vision is 20/20
even if you can't
physically see
love is the greatest
compass but
sometimes love is blind
so the blind lead the blind
I wish I wasn't blind
I wish I could see
like Stevie

Truth Is a Lie

beautiful lies
running out of time
i'm only 33 but i'm
empty
emptiness embraces
wholeness
wholeness is nothing
nothing is everything
and i'm tired of that
everything is weary
everyone is weary
i like feeling empty
emptiness is appropriate
for the times
feeling whole in the
present feels
like a sin
emptiness is king
wholeness is queen
but I'm just a
fucking man
yin yang
balance
imbalance
love
hate
sighs
cries
laughter
screams
silence
go ahead
laugh at my pain
i don't fucking care

it's all funny
i know this
truth is a lie too
fuck my feelings
my emotional state
needs a good lay
lay down, ego
lay down, hope
you need to be
put in your place
and so do i
whatever i is
stop the maniacs
stop the sane
for they are one
and the same
one is a wolf in sheeps
clothing and the other is
a sheep in wolfs clothing
dying to be set free
i lie a lot but then
again
truth
is
a
lie
too
so
fuck
you
if
you
judge
Me

BURNT OUT

I'm tired
I'm fried
My circuits are
Broken
My life is boring
I'm sick of school
All of the homework
I'm burnt out
Tired of my vices
Heavy prices.
Wisdom is priceless
Time is timeless
Dont want the virus
Really anxious
Not a wankster
Not a prankster
Not a gangster
I'm tired
Could someone
Help me
I want to be free
Cant be in this
Society

A Broken Hallelujah

The
Nonsensical
Makes sense
To me.
My love is
Fading
And getting
Stronger
Every day.
Strength is
Overrated.
Getting by
Is all we can
Do sometimes.
Vulnerable persistence.
Weak love.
Broken hallelujahs
Are more important
Than strength.
But then again,
Maybe they are one
And the same.
A broken hallelujah
Is all I can muster.
But maybe that's
Enough.

I Truly Loved Her

I truly loved her.
The best I knew how.
What is love?
If my experience of
Love is a lie,
Then what is the point?
I guess truth is the point,
If it exists.
What is truth?
Does anyone really know
Or are they only
Educated guesses?
What is beautiful without
Love and truth?
Especially if you don't know
what they are?
I truly loved her
I think.
I walked with her for
Two years.

She walked with me.
But I was sick.
If she truly loved me
Would she have stayed
Despite the shit I put
Her through?
I truly loved her
But I was sick.
She was beautiful.
I guess she still is.
I wouldn't know.
Now she has a child.
And a husband who
Isn't me.
A piece of me will
Always love her.
But what is love?
I did my best.
I truly loved her.
I think.

REALISTIC HOPE

Life is a game
That no one makes
It out of alive.
Anxiety from the virus.
Imprisoned in my own home.
Love is somewhat
Irrelevant right now.
We're all just trying
To make it through this
Pandemic alive.
So love is a luxury
I can barely afford.
Hope is a choice.
I choose hope.
As realistic as possible.
Sometimes you have to
Force it even though
Realism and hope
Are not synonymous
Right now.
During hard times,
Forcing your next two steps
Is all that you can really do.
One foot in front of the other.
Minute by minute.
The seconds go by slowly.
Its not time to give up
Even though the temptation
To is great.
We will make it.
Many will die but most
Will survive.
Hold on to your
Reasons for living
And never give up
No matter what.
Even if your only hope
Is trying to find a reason to
hope,
For that is hope in and of itself
And is more than enough.
So keep hoping,
Realistically.

[It's dark in my room]

It's dark in my room
Despite the light
Its 6:40 am
I can feel the light
Of morning
Even though I
Cant see it
Light and dark
A competition
Of the ages
Maybe more of a
Collaboration
Cant have one
Without
The
Other
My lungs are scarred
From smoking
My soul is scarred
From persisting
My love is scarred
From heartbreak
Still
I
Rise

The End of the World (revised)

Who knew that the
End of the world
Would be like this?
Screaming.
People are jumping
Out of buildings.
People are still being
Killed by police-
But not in the
public eye.
Nothing new
in that regard.
I witnessed a
murder the other
Day.
Someone shot and
Killed someone else
On the bus.
There is rape
In the news.
There have been
Many suicides.
These things
Are in the news.
There is nothing new
except they have increased.
But the greatest noise is
Being caused by a
Silent killer.
There is just Covid-19.
And there is silence.
There is silence.
Just silence.
What do you feel?
What do you hear?
What do you see?
I see a ghost town.
I feel extreme anxiety.
But all I hear is
Silence above
Everything else.

And the music on
my computer.
My computer cannot
Drown out all of the
Noise.
The silence is
Deafening.
Who knew that the end
Of the world would
Be like this.
Going out in
Silent pain.
I believe we'll make
It through
But perhaps this
Is how the world will
end when it does.
A silent panic.
A soft drowning
With water filling up
Our lungs in a polluted
Stupor of Covid virus.
Distance from one
Another.
Keep 6 feet away.
No hugs.
No handshakes.
No kisses.
Just love from a
Distance.
Then more silence.
If I die I will go out
With hope and a
Cigarette in my mouth.
I believe we'll make it
Through.
But who would've thought
That the world would end
In
Silence.

Paralyzed

My anxiety is crippling.
I feel its intensity.
Where is my hope?
Where is my drive?
I'm paralyzed.
What happened to
Moving forward?
What happened to
The finish line?
What happened to
The light at the end
of the tunnel?
All I see is a
50 foot wall
Blocking my path.
I hate feeling this way.
Self sabotage.
Subconscious sabotage.
I feel like I cant move.
I cant do what I need to do.
I don't want to do
What I need to do.
There is a great weight
On top of my being.
Heavy depression.
I'm tired of
Fighting myself.
I'm tired of fighting.
I'm tired.
I'm my own
Worst enemy.
Purgatory.
I'm paralyzed.

WHAT I'M MADE OF

Stuck on a hamster wheel.
What do I have to do to
Feel anything but pain?
I think I like it that way.
Pain is easier than
Feeling good for me.
I like the challenge.
Sometimes I hate the challenge.
But I like having
Something to hate.
I'm so full of shit.
Maybe I like it that way.
It gives me an excuse to fuck
up.
That's real.
I'm a dying breed,
Although I'm not really sure
What breed I am.
Maybe that's why I write poetry.
To find out what I'm made of.
I've never been this depressed
On such a beautiful, sunny day.
That's a lie.
I've been much more depressed
Before while watching the
Cloudless sky.
Ive barely held on
But I'm used to that.
I'm still hanging on.
That is the important thing.
Wait, what is the important
thing?
I really don't know but
I have some ideas.
Truth.

Beauty.
Love.
Trust.
Spirituality.
Maybe even God.
But what happens when
Those are no longer enough?
Then what do you do?
I'm lost and found
At the same damn time.
Who am I?
Who am i without my talent
And hopefulness?
Who am i without my anxiety
And depression?
Who am i, period?
Who do i turn to
when i need help?
Who can help me?
Can anyone?
Am i a problem that
Will never be solved?
Am I a solution that
doesn't need its problem?
Solutions can be lost too
If they don't know what part
Of their problems and assets
Make them
Who they are.
What is truth?
What is MY truth?
What is THE truth?
I want to know what
I'm made of.

Never Give Up

I'm hanging in there.
My love is strong.
My hope is in tact.
My belief is weak,
but I refuse to give up.
I'm doing the best I can
and I can do better.
The dialectal
dream.
Many things can
be true at the same time.
I'm hanging in there.
The sky is blue today.
My mind is hazy.
But my persistence
is strong.
Never give up.
I'm behind in school
but I'm still trying.
Don't give up until the end,
even if you fail.
You will have not failed
if you gave it your all.
I hope I don't fail.
Fail is an interesting word.
Someone I knew used
to say there are no losers.
Just winners and learners.
I refuse to give up.
Anxiety and depression
are strong.
The sky is blue today
outside but internally
I'm a little hazy and overcast.
My higher power,
please help me to do the best
that I can,
and also to do better
at the same time.
I am learning
patiently to love myself.
You will not lose if
you never give up.

Breathe Eternal

Beautiful people.
Horrible virus.
Beat the virus.
Long live the people.
Sitting on red cotton.
A regular guy feeling
holy as I write down
my sins and painful
regularities.
Beating up myself.
My self is winning.
And simultaneously
Losing.
If you do both then
you transcend both.
Transcendence over
everything.
Be in the moment.
Breathe.
Breathe through the times.
Love through the aches.
Sing through the silence.
Love the most
unlovable parts of
yourself.

Because the killer in me
is the killer in you.
The saint in me
is the saint in you.
The average, regular
man in me is the
ordinary version of you.
Approach death with love
For when you transition
from your body,
the love will fly above
and will remain eternal.
What is eternal
will remain eternal,
for it is eternal.
What is eternal in me
is eternal in you.
To love the best in you,
you must love the worst in you.
Amidst the negative chatter,
Always listen to the broken
hallelujah,
the voice that refuses to give
up.
Broken Hallelujah forever.

Alive

I feel hope.
I feel not
what I used
to feel.
Help me to
feel something.
Anything.
I like feeling.
I like the pain.
I like the joy.
I like the mixed
states of being.
I love life.
I like myself.
I love myself
even when I
hate myself.
I like
being
alive.

Anti-Profundity

Life is a beautiful
Symphony and
All of that other
Crap us poets
Like to say.
But I'm tired
Of that.
I want to say
Something beautiful
But perhaps the only
beautiful things
that are left
are ironically
The non beautiful.
I want to write
A profound poem
But it seems
As though the
Profound is dead.
Is the opposite of
Profound just the
Mundane or is it

Reality?
I'm tired of
Talking about reality.
I'm also tired of talking
About the profound.
Is a truly original
Piece possible?
What are the pieces
That we put together
To form it?
What are the spaces
In between?
How do you compose
A masterpiece?
I'm tired of the
Questions.
I'm tired of trying.
Charles Bukowski
Said "Don't Try."
Perhaps I'll try that
For awhile.

I See Boxes: An Ode to Gratitude

I see boxes
in my moms
apartment.
There is a lot
of space
and a lot of
light.
It's very
nice.
I'm sitting
with my mother
as I hear the news
of my grandfathers
impending death.
He's 94 and he has
the virus.
Covid is a killer,
especially when
you're of old age.
He's lived a long life.

A good life.
I see the light in
this living room of
my moms and I think
about him having to
die alone in quarantine.
I'm grateful for the light
while I can still see it.
I'm grateful for the air
while I can still breathe it.
I'm grateful for the music
I'm listening to while
I can still hear it.
I'm grateful for being with my
mother in this beautiful space
while I can still be with her.
I'm grateful for the light
as it cascades through
our experience.

Simple Nothings

Simplify.
A theory of
Everything.
Bridging the
Gap to nothing
With an
Elegant
Equation
To make
Sense
Of the big
And small.
Transcend
Into
Empty
Space.
Emptiness
Is
Everything.

Numbers, Notes, and Beauty

Symmetry.

Numbers

Of the

Universe.

Come together

And form

The truth.

What is true

Is what is

Beautiful.

Less is more.

Truth in an

Elegant

Equation

Will never

Disappoint.

Coltrane and

Gershwin.

Show me

Their numbers

And I will

Show you

What is

Beautiful.

VIBRATIONS

Beauty.
Subjectivity.
Uncontrollability.
Spaces between notes.
Notes between space.
Vast galaxies stretch
Outward quickly.
Imagination is more
Important than
Knowledge.
Imagination is more
Potent than
Knowledge.
A symphony of
What we know and
What we can
Imagine.
Space between
Nothing and
Infinity.
They are the same.
Spaces between notes.
Space between the stars.

Vibrating strings.
Vibrating minds.
Vibrating times.
Vibrating crimes.
It's all beautiful.
Light and dark.
One cannot be
Without the other.
Nietzsche said,
We must have chaos
Within us to give birth
To a dancing star.
Vibrations are the key.
All creation is chaotic.
Just because I can't see
You anymore doesn't mean
You're not there.
I will always feel
Your vibration.
I'm grateful for that.
And the universe
Expands.

Send Me an Angel

Love is a losing game.
One I love to play.
Someone has to lose
in every game.
Sometimes the love
lasts whole lives.
There are many injuries.
Give and take.
Til death do us part.
Perhaps I will find
my soul mate,
one who I will be
willing to get injured by.
And to be healed by.
Perhaps I have already
met her.
Love is a losing game.
One I am willing to play
with the right person.
I'm ready to win at love.
Please send her to me.
Send me an angel.
To carry me home.
Cuz I don't want to
walk alone.

NONSENSICAL SENSIBILITY

Scary times.
Sinful crimes.
Blissful ties
to complex lies.
You said you would
tell me the truth but
I doubt it because that
too was a lie.
A loving bind.
Still moving though
I'm blind.
Truth I will find
if you don't mind.
I will always try
even if its amidst
my teary cries.
I try to rhyme
though it makes
me sigh.
Rhyming is overrated,
Why?
If love is blind then
why did I commit the crime
of breaking up with her
this time?
I miss her as I cry.
She is no longer in my life.
Though I've lived through strife,

I put down my knife
and realize that she won't
ever be my wife.
Timeless time.
It goes by so slowly
so I choose to unwind.
Writing nonsense on the page.
Nonsensical wisdom is the best.
I lay bare my chest,
say do your best to destroy me.
I write another poem then I rest.
I struggle with demons but I'm
also blessed.
Stressed by life's trials and tests.
But I'm not that mad about it
because
I know that I'm one of the only
real ones left.
Feel my realness in the heart
grown inside your chest.
For your heart is like a long lost
treasure chest.
And life is like a long game of
chess.
Loving blessings.
Long live nonsensical bliss
and life's hard lessons.

Rhyming Experiment #1

Lazy eye

Crazy times.

Lifting cries.

Shortage spies.

Taking flight.

Loving life.

Poster child.

Poets strife.

Making love.

Praying tough.

Life is rough.

Soar above.

Spirit dove.

You're enough.

Lovers quarrel.

Mothers aura.

Fathers saintly.

Prayers are rhythm.

Rhythm treble.

Music faintly.

Horror fainting.

Spirit chanting.

Love ornately.

Wizard spelling.

Chisel music.

Never breaking.

Lever pulling.

Water flowing

You're creating.

More cleverly.

Vast debating.

Masked creation.

Fears the nation.

Cheers to bravery.

Passion poetry.

Clashing soft

And witty.

Words of nonsense.

Oh so pretty.

Make a wish.

Beautiful city.

I Must Persist

My mind is torn
apart but I
must persist.
Through the valleys
of depression and
the mountains of
anxiety.
They were an unstoppable
force until they met my soul.
What a battle between
my trials and tribulations.
My being is stronger.
I'm tough even when I'm soft.
Two unstoppable forces collide
then they transcend to
form my art.
Demons versus the phoenix.
The eternal war.
The good will win
as long as we still believe.
Faith in goodness will always win
even if we lose many battles.
Its existence is enough.
As long as we are alive
and believing,
we will always have a good
chance to win the war.
Always believe,
even when you don't.

Phoenix

There is a phoenix
caged in my being.
I inhale cigarette smoke
to cover him up.
I let him out sometimes
late at night.
Then I force him back down
into my depths.
From the ashes of
my essence he would rise
if only I would let him.
The phoenix tries to rise every day
and then I shove him down
and say get back down there.
I can't let the world see you.
Your beauty is too much
for the world to believe in.
I suffocate him with
cigarette smoke.
I drown him with Coca Cola.
The world is not ready to
see you Phoenix.
But you still rise every day
as much as my insecurities
will let you.
There's a phoenix in my being,
and he rises when I write.
That's the only time I let him.
I know why the caged bird sings.
Maybe one day I'll let him free.
When the world is ready.
Or maybe when I'm ready.
I guess we'll see.

Rhyme Experiment #2

Trusting toughness.

Raging softness.

Loving kindness.

Horrid Blindness.

Wisdom timeless.

Freedom shrineless.

Money dimeless.

Honey priceless.

Worldly martyrs.

Brainy psychics.

Voice is mic'd up.

World a psych ward.

Life is so hard.

Glass shards.

Fat broads.

Half cup.

Movin up.

Rhymes wassup.

Stinging wasps.

Singing costs.

Soul is bought.

Love is taught.

Hope is naught.

A LOT OF POEMS

I've written a lot of poems.
I've felt a lot of different emotions.
I've seen a lot of beautiful sights.
I've heard a lot of beautiful sounds.
I've had a lot of beautiful women.
What does it all amount to?
What does it all mean?
What if it meant nothing?
I've lived through a lot of hardship.
I've experienced psychosis.
I've inspired many people.
I've hurt many people.
Learning to love myself
where I'm at is the key.
What if there was no reason
for loving myself?
No reward for doing whats right.
Doing what's right is enough
in and of itself.
Write beautiful words
and go all of the way.
Love yourself even when
you hate yourself.
Be the meaning where
there is no meaning.
Go all of the way.
Faith is an interesting thing.
You can believe even if you
know not what you believe in.
That is the nature of the phoenix.
That is the nature of the paradox
called dialectical life.

I FEEL ALIVE

I feel alive.
There is nothing
Better than
Feeling alive.
I feel the heat
Between us.
I see the sparks.
Are we just friends?
Are we more?
I'm ok with not knowing.
I like being with you.
I like our bond.
Our friendship is strong.
I don't mind either way.
But I feel alive.
My music.
My poetry.
The heat.
The passion.
The love.
Between us.
There is something there.
I know it.
What it is only time
Will tell.
I like the journey.
I'll go there with you.
Friendship first,
Maybe more later.
But the point is,
You make me feel
Alive.

POPPY

The enigmatic one.
The hilarious one.
The beautiful one.
The brave one.
The great one.
He saw what no
Human being should
Ever see at a young age.
Walking skeletons
Coming out of Buchenwald,
The demonic concentration
camp.
A forward observer.
Witnessing hell on earth
During World War II.
He came home and met his
love.
Evelyn Goldman. Nama.
They bravely started a family.
Believing in the good despite
Seeing the hellish disciples
Almost take over the world.
My mom, their first child.

I am alive because of them.
He joked and laughed through
life.
Funny as hell.
Loving life despite what he'd
seen.
We would always go eat Chi-
nese
Together.
We talked about music and
whoever
I was dating at the time.
Beautiful women in general.
Great times.
A beautiful man.
A strong, charismatic soul.
He will always be.
I cant see him anymore
But his vibration is eternal.
Transitioning to the life after life.
You will never be forgotten.
I love you forever.

WHERE DO THE SPIRITS GO?

Where do the spirits go?

Do they go home?

Where is home?

I don't see it

But I feel the vibration.

There is a vibration that

Never dies.

When the body dies,

Where do the spirits go?

Do they go home?

Where is home?

I hope one day to go.

Long live the spirit.

Forever we will float.

Vibrate on

Righteous brother.

Vibrate on.

DEADENED LEAVES

Deadened leaves
Press close to
My sleeveless shirt.
I'm scared of life
More than death.
Death will be a relief.
When the time comes.
Until then I still believe.
Dead end streets
Fill with lost souls
Screaming at one
Another.
But they are really
Screaming at themselves.
The darkness is too much
So they take it out on
Each other.
I am not immune
To the emptiness.
Crashing into other
Humans briefly fills
The void.
We must crash if we don't
Know how to love.
Deadened leaves press
Close to my sleeveless shirt.
I am like those leaves.
I'd like to find inner peace.
To be at ease.
But I crash into myself
Sometimes because I
Don't know how to love.
I crash into myself
Then I yell at a
Stranger.

Ricocheting Images

Ricocheting images
Of love.
Where does it come from?
I'm in a glass house.
A hall of mirrors.
Who do I trust?
What should I believe?
There is more to life
Than what you can achieve.
What is the original source?
How can I know when all I see
Is different angles of my reflection?
Being bombarded by opinions.
Everyone has one.
Living life and feeling alive
While I'm at it.
I'm on fire.
What reflected angle is really me?
Perhaps all of the above
Is me.
Every echo, every reflection,
Every poem, every opinion.
I am large.
I contain multitudes.
The blank page is my
Greatest friend.
I create my own freedom
And my own misery.
I can feel my spirit
Through it all.
Enigmatic me.
I can feel the truth even if I
Don't know what to believe.

Something to Believe In

Beauty is beautiful.
It is hard to find.
Love is good.
I'm running out of time.
No one knows how
long they have to live.
Positivity just might
be overrated.
My soul is livid.
Happiness is a hard
emotion to live in.
But we still strive
for something to
believe in.
The pursuit of
happiness is free
but i'll take some
money to live with.
My love is strong.
My feelings are stronger.
Depression is the
silent killer.
I will overcome

these emotions.
When I write,
I feel like I'm living
in slow motion.
Anything to make
the time last longer.
Writing helps me
beat my demons.
Sometimes
I fly when I express
these words on paper.
There is a pheonix
in my heart and he
will live as long as
I write.
God Bless You
and yours.
Do what makes
you feel alive.
And never lose
respect for your life.

Ash, Soda Bottles, and Cigarette Butts

Laying on my bed.
Surrounded by ash,
Soda bottles filled
With cigarette butts.
An Edgar Kunz
Poetry book called Tap Out,
A book called The Wisdom
Of Psychopaths laying
On my bed with me as
I contemplate mortality.
Books on my shelves
And clothes scattered
Across the floor.
I haven't sat at my desk
To write in some time
But I will always write.
I have the right.
And thank god for that,
Who or whatever God is.
I look at my junked room
And it screams starving
Artist- underrated writer,
Musician.

I channel Charles Bukowski
As I revel in defeat.
It has only made me stronger.
A shitty life will not stop me
From writing good shit
With my pen.
Fuck societies opinion
Of anything.
What do they know anyway?
I've already battled with Goliath
From the gates of hell and back.
But guess what?
My Hebrew name is Dovid.
I will always believe like David.
Throw me to the wolves.
Shit on my art.
Reduce me to the temporary
Nature of defeat.
But at the end of the day
I will still rise and
Defeat goliath.

Dialectical Colors

Black and white
thinking.
It is bigger than
black and white.
The dialectic
reality is a beautiful one.
It's never as simple as
two colors.
There is a whole spectrum-
a rainbow.
There is good in the worst
and the worst in the best.
I'm grateful for colors
that I can see
and in my emotions.
I feel in color
and in rhyme.
It's only a matter of
time before I shine.
I'm shining now.
I'm on fire but
my soul is blue.
My happiness too is
the color blue.

I transcend my anger
with exercise.
My demons still try
but I know that they lie.
Love is a dream.
And dialectically a reality.
Blue will always
defy the red.
And sometimes they
mix and create
the color purple-
still a beautiful color.
I am not afraid of the
spectrum of light
or the spectrum of my
emotions.
I've been through it all.
I will never give up.
I know that you can
persist and resist too.
And live in the color blue.

MESHUGGENAH

THE NOTES OF A WEATHERED SYMPHONY

Love has seasons
Like the weather.
I'm listening to
Classical music
And wanting to
Write something
Beautiful that
Fits the complexity
Of what I'm hearing.
I'm wanting to talk about
The seasons in a year
As beautifully as the notes
Of this symphony.
I want to describe the notes
Of the weathered landscape
In all of its diversity, its cultured
And colored simplicity.
Life is a symphony.
Complex like all of
the different notes.
The notes are just right.
The fall is like a cello.
A deeply beautiful
Death of the spring
And the summer making
Us cry with its rigid bass.
The winter is like a piano
Cold and ivory keys press

Down gracefully like the
snow from the sky.
The summer is a gorgeous,
Light melody that inspires
Dancing on the guitar.
The spring is like a drum
Played expertly, beating
rhythm
And newly born life like the
Leaves growing on the trees.
The weather is creative
Like the music of our lives.
I love the seasons like the
notes
Of a perfectly planned piece of
Professionally performed pa-
nache music.
The beautiful instruments put
pained
But gorgeous melodies togeth-
er
To perform a symphony as
complex
As love, death, and rebirth
That we feel in the notes of our
Hearts.

104

Impressionist Lyricism

Impressionist lyricism.
Out of control medicine.
Underrated talent.
Unloved lover.
Lover of the unloved.
Pretty rhymes.
Running out of time.
Competitiveness
Unmatched.
Mortal beauty.
Dead soul.
Nerves on fire.
Ready to die.
Ready to live.
Should I die before
I wake
Give me the truth
On a blank page of
Empty lies.
Lift up the body
Of reckless work.
Lazy discipline.
Less didactic.
More impressionist.
Lover of lies disguised

As a beautiful painting.
Dead dreams unmatched
With a modern terrorism
Of love.
Love is a lie.
We lie because we love.
Fuck love.
Empty wholeness.
Forgotten nightmares.
Bloody truths
Self-evident on a
Stage of bullshit.
Raging against a machine
That will never die.
Timeless truths.
Timeless lies.
Timeless cries.
Timeless time.
Fuck time.
Time killed my sister.
I believe in the life
I stopped living
When she died.
Impressionist lyricism
Forever.

THANK YOU FOR READING MY WRITTEN WORKS!

Made in the USA
Monee, IL
05 June 2022

97481251R00059